How to Become A Successful Virtual Assistant

Jeanie Halpert

Table of Contents

Who is a Virtual Assistant?

A VA is a hired strategic partner that offers value and makes their client's life simpler by delivering administrative, creative, and technological aid. Some of the most typical tasks of a VA include research, calendar and time management, verbal, visual, and written communication, travel bookings, email management, data entry, and presentations. VAs may also have particular expertise, such as social media management or event organizing.

Simply put, a virtual assistant makes their client's life easier.

Think of it this way: a small business owner needs assistance managing the ins and outs of her company (from maintaining the company's Facebook page, to getting her finances under control). There's too much to do, but too little time – and that's when they engage virtual assistance to help.

Being a virtual assistant doesn't always imply you'll be an executive assistant. You will not always conduct standard administrative activities like managing monthly costs in Excel or scheduling meetings (unless that's what you specialize in, of course).

In most situations, virtual assistants are self-employed and operate as independent contractors, and it's normal for VAs to work for many customers at once.

People recruited as virtual assistants usually have several years of experience as administrative assistants or office managers. New options are opening up for virtual assistants who are adept in social media, content management, blog post writing, graphic design, and internet marketing. As working from home has become increasingly acceptable for both individuals and organizations, the need for professional virtual assistants is set to rise.

Perks of being a Virtual Assistant

One of the best things about this role is that it is so diverse. Depending on who you work with, one day, you may be generating a newsletter and organizing Facebook postings, the next day, you may be organizing a start-up conference in Paris. Yes, truly.

And – since it's virtual – you may be anywhere in the globe while helping someone keep their firm on track. Yes, you may even be in Paris yourself.

Working in your PJs, not paying for parking, not eating the same drab store-bought sandwich for lunch – and, maybe most critically, being there to take your dog out for a walk... These are some of the fantastic perks of virtual assistant work.

There are various strategies to produce money from home, but working as a virtual assistant offers the appropriate balance of being practical and satisfying. It doesn't need much knowledge, merely a basic set of talents you can gain rapidly.

It's also a superb technique to get into the realm of freelancing – and boost your abilities as well as understand anything about online business.

Why Virtual Assistant?

There are several reasons why folks strive to become Virtual assistants. The key ones are flexibility and freedom, but here are a few more:

You can work when you choose

From being able to spend more time with your kids to caring for senior family members, working as a Virtual Assistant means you may tailor your day to fit around the life you have or the type of life you want to develop.

You can work where you choose

I've worked from places all around the globe since all I need is my laptop and an Internet connection. If you're pursuing a location-independent or digital nomad lifestyle, virtual help will meet the bill perfectly.

You get to employ yourself

Working by yourself is a continuously expanding experience that requires you to think for yourself and come up with new ideas for both your own firm and your clients'.

It's gratifying

Dedicating years of your life to a business that doesn't appreciate you or honor your passion and hard work is heartbreaking. But, when you manage your own Virtual Assistant service, it's you who's rewarded – both financially and emotionally.

You finally get to see what you're made of and what you can do.

The Much Needed Skills

While the talents and services you supply as a virtual assistant vary a lot, certain required qualities would make the task simpler, more engaging, and more delightful.

A well-rounded VA must have a diverse combination of good soft and technical talents. Let's take a minute to study the two.

Soft Skills

These are talents, attitudes, and habits that help a person prosper in the profession. They are beneficial in nearly any work and are not restricted to a particular purpose. That suggests that regardless of what vocation you choose in the future, you will require a robust set of soft skills. Soft skills are often referred to as professional skills.

- Self-management
- Discretion and Confidentiality
- Organizational skills
- Grit & Growth Mindset
- Resourcefulness
- Communication skills
- Emotional Intelligence
- Proactiveness
- Staying cool under pressure
- Accuracy
- Adaptability
- Patience
- Prioritization
- Problem-solving
- Time Management

- People Skills
- Self-awareness
- Anticipating Client's Needs

Technical Skills

These pertain to particular abilities and knowledge necessary to execute a certain activity. They enable you to be productive and efficient in your job. They are straightforward to assess or evaluate and may be strengthened by study and practice. Technical talents are frequently referred to as hard skills.

- Internet Research
- Authoring successful surveys
- Transcribing

- Managing a client's inbox
- Data input & expenditure tracking
- Attending to customers
- Travel reservations
- Creating meeting agendas
- Project management
- Taking meeting minutes
- Writing correspondence
- Managing a client's calendar
- Scheduling
- Stakeholder management
- Creating presentations
- Labeling and Filing
- Creating travel itineraries

Since you'll be working online, having a broad knowledge of all-things-internet is crucial. Don't get me wrong - no one is expecting you to be an IT specialist, but you will need to have some technical talents to perform activities like writing a blog post, managing social media, or producing a PDF.

To make you more desirable to a prospective customer (and allow you the ability to charge more for your VA service), it also helps if you have special expertise or two to offer. For example, you may investigate and comprehend all there is to know about the Facebook platform. Then, you may specialize as a Facebook Virtual Assistant, charging a bigger price for your specialized ability.

If you have minimal employment experience or don't know how to execute these things today, don't worry. You may learn them reasonably simply with online lessons or free videos.

Many abilities may be developed on the job and added to your portfolio as you go.

Much Needed Tools

Over and beyond having great wifi and laptop, tools refer to software packages (or apps) you need to be able to use to do various duties. Each technical ability is tightly related to a certain set of applications. Most customers or companies employ Google Workspace or Microsoft Office (MS) products. Some clientele utilize Apple iWork.

Here is a broad variety of abilities and tools that a VA generally requires. Please read through each one. Do any stick out for you? Are there abilities and tools you are already competent in?

- Google Forms
- MS Word

- MS Outlook (email and calendar)
- Gmail
- Google Slides
- Box
- MS Forms
- Google Meet
- Trello
- MS Excel
- Zoom
- Google Calendar
- Google Drive
- Asana
- MS OneNote
- Google Docs
- Google Sheets
- MS PowerPoint

How Should You Charge?

If you're asking yourself, "how much does a virtual assistant earn per hour?", the reality is that the wage range ranges widely and relies on your competence and your customer.

One of the most attractive elements about being a freelance virtual assistant is that you are the boss – meaning, you select how much to charge your customers for your VA service.

That said, if you wake up one morning and decide you want to become a freelance writer or graphic designer without any skills, you won't be able to charge hundreds of dollars straight instantly. Building a VA firm needs time, relationships, and recommendations to identify the suitable consumer.

If you don't have much relevant experience, your beginning compensation per hour will be relatively modest (and can be below $10 an hour).

However, if you have some experience and a great website that helps emphasize your talents and knowledge, you may be making as much as $35+ an hour (without leaving your house!).
Sounds lovely, right?

Two pricing techniques will be examined in this book.

Method 1

Step 1

Decide if you want to work per hour (monthly retainer) or job.

Per hour: This is for individuals that want your services for a period of time (monthly basis). They have responsibilities that need ongoing attention and need you to labor for at least 3 hours. Retainer clients generally earn a lesser charge as they operate with you for a lengthy length of time. You are paid for the hours you work and have to employ a task tracker (e.g Asana) so your customer only pays you for active hours.

Per project: You get reimbursed for a given project. So you work with the customer till their project is complete and get paid for it. This can take hours, weeks, or months. So you'll price the whole thing in a single cost with the knowledge, time, and software essential to accomplish the job in mind. For example, you may work with a customer for a product launch and when their product is out, your job is done. I propose you take at least 50 percent of the entire cost before you start and the remainder when the service is done.

Per Package: You package a bundle of skills/services and assign a price to it. This is my preferred strategy to billing my services as using the hourly pricing technique, you get paid less if you can accomplish the work quickly (you get punished for being quicker than a lazy/slow

VA). But with packages, you can convince customers to pay you based on your knowledge and the outcomes you give (and maintain your services) instead of a one-off.

Step 2

Get a notepad and answer the following questions.

How much do you want to make per month? Now increase how much you want to make each month by 12 to obtain your income objective for the year.

How many weeks are you willing to work each year? I think 40 - 44 weeks is suitable.

How many days are you willing to work every month?

How many hours are you willing to work every day?

How many consumers can you manage per month?

How much does operating your firm cost you every month? (Consider your monthly data subscription, paid subscription for training, tools, software, etc.)

How much value are you delivering your clients? (Not all services are of similar value. Web design costs more than email administration).

How much are other VAs (your competition) charging for the same services? If you charge too cheap, you'll be misleading yourself and some clients may assume your services are sub-standard. And if you price your services excessively, people won't select you for obvious reasons. You have to identify your price sweet spot (= what works best for you and your ideal buyer.

Step 3

Decide on the Number of Clients You Need to Achieve that Goal.

Can you get one customer that can pay you for all the hours you desire to work for the month (depending on your hourly rate)? Then one consumer is fine. Depending on your garage of talents, you might have to attract 4 customers who will pay you a specified money each to fulfill your income objective, and allocate your hours among them.

Don't forget that your target consumers' income affects the amount of money they are prepared to spend for your services.

Method 2

You may price your services depending on what is accessible in the industry. To get an idea of how much people are ready to pay for the services you're thinking of giving, or how much VAs are asking, for the services selling like hot cakes around them, then ask!

I'm always willing to tell you how much I charge if it's a service I provide or I'm familiar with. After setting your price, go out there and look for your ideal clients.

Hot Virtual Assistant Services

While the type of work you conduct as a virtual assistant varies and will rely on elements like your skill set, your speciality, hobbies, former career, and even region - certain services are in higher demand than others.

Offering several separate services suggests that your consumers won't have to outsource to several freelancers, making their lives easier and you – a more enticing alternative.

Remember I indicated that you may give a number of services as a virtual assistant? The trick is, it is preferable to give a selection of services particularly when you are just starting. What you are aiming to do is test the waters and discover what you like and what you should expand on.

Whatever you choose, there's always a market for it. All you have to do is put yourself out there and tell people what you do.

Here's a list of top services virtual assistants deliver that people pay for:

Email Management

No one appreciates seeing thousands of unopened emails in their inbox. Honestly, sometimes it becomes too much, and I'm tempted to mistakenly push "archive all" — and pretend I never got them.

But that's not a rational decision. Instead, why not engage someone to keep on top of your inbox? And that's precisely what individuals may engage a virtual assistant to aid with.

Administrative Support

Admin tasks are relatively straightforward - they are likely most directly related with virtual assistant jobs. Administrative assistant help may include:Booking appointments and calls, Making travel arrangements, Preparing PowerPoint presentations and so on.

Customer Service

The most popular virtual assistant employment is inside customer service. Keeping consumers delighted is crucial to

any small company that wants to flourish –
but it demands a huge time investment.

And company owners don't have that much
time on their hands – which is why they
employ fantastic people like you and pay
you to make their lives easy.

Content Production

Businesses need exceptional content to
generate and keep engagement with their
audiences.

Offering content development services may
offer you a competitive advantage over other
virtual assistants.

Finance Management

Staying on top of money is something that a
lot of people require assistance with –

whether that's personal finances, corporate finances – or both. If you have some expertise in this subject and get on with numbers, you may give financial management services to your consumer

Outreach

Building relationships and improving awareness is crucial for every firm – if they want to develop a valuable brand. And, although there are several techniques to enhance your exposure as a firm, they are very time-consuming – which is why organizations may employ a virtual assistant to take care of it.

Social Media Management

Being a virtual assistant isn't only about spreadsheets and other shipping orders! If you know (or are willing to learn) how to maintain social media accounts, organizations will employ you as they require assistance with it. Being active on social media as a corporation is vitally essential nowadays – but creating a solid social media presence, again, needs a big-time commitment and some specialist expertise.

This is why company owners may outsource social media management responsibilities to individuals who know more about it than them. Also if you concentrate on one distinct specialization, you could locate bigger consumers who are ready to pay extra for unique platform knowledge.

Online Marketing

With a huge percentage of the U.S. population being online (with the number of internet users always rising!), most organizations need to do everything they can to boost the performance of their online marketing.

Connecting with audiences is the primary purpose of every organization - providing they want to sell their product or service, of course. Having skills in the online marketing industry would signify you're greatly regarded as a virtual assistant.

Email Marketing

While some marketers are suggesting that email marketing is dead, stats indicate that's far from reality. Not only are there over 5.6

billion active email accounts globally but the U.S. is estimated to spend 350 million dollars on email advertising in 2019.

Website/ Blog Management

Many companies now hand over the management of their website and/or blog to virtual assistants. So, if you know your way around WordPress, this may be a wonderful service to add to your VA firm offering.

If you don't know anything about WordPress yet, there's loads of content accessible.

Becoming a Virtual Assistant

So, now that you know a bit more about what working as a virtual assistant may be like, you may be wondering what steps you'd need to complete to get started.

First, let me tell you something: if you worry about a lack of relevant job experience - don't. As I've indicated earlier, you don't need years of knowledge to get started – but you do need to be clear about what you want your VA firm to look like.

1. Decide On Your Services

The first stage in how to become a virtual assistant is getting clear about what types of services you'll supply.

It may be good to assess the talents you have and compare them to the services a virtual assistant may supply.

Maybe you operate your website or blog or know how to edit images for social media remarkably well. Maybe you're the master of sophisticated Excel calculations that can simplify someone's finances with the push of a button.

Spend some time thinking about what you're exceptional at – and would like to accomplish. Compare what your abilities are vs. what others need aid with – and pick what services your VA business will give.

Your services, of course, will not need to conclude there – as you'll continually add new talents (as well as, say, apps you're comfortable with) as you advance in your career as a successful virtual assistant.

Eventually, knowing how you may give value to your clients, and what your unique selling points (USP) features are, is a prudent first step towards success.

2. Decide how much you're going to charge

As noted above, how much you charge for your services will rely on your skill set, experience, and the type of services you decided to give.

If you're someone who has a great lot of organizational experience or has previously worked as an assistant, you shouldn't be scared to ask for a larger remuneration per hour.

However, if you're new to being an assistant and are wanting to build up your portfolio and abilities, you may need to start on the lower end of the range to attract more customers and develop experience.

A handful of key elements to bear in mind while establishing your pricing are:

You'll need to pay self-employment tax, so make sure that whatever you charge pays for that;
By becoming a virtual assistant you'll also gain other fees, such as website hosting, software subscriptions, and office expenditures – so make sure you take these

in mind when determining how much to charge.

Lastly, there are no benefits. No paid vacation, no sick days, no health insurance. Should things go wrong, you'll need to cover it out of your pocket.

It's vital to take all of that in mind when calculating your prices. No matter how much of a rookie you are, be sure you don't land up in debt because you're severely undercharging your consumers.

The way around that is to think about how much you'd make if you were to conduct the equivalent task in an office — then add 25 percent to counterbalance the costs. It isn't surprising that freelancers often make more than workers — when you think about how many more considerations there are to take into account.

I recognize that creating reasonable rates and communicating to your customers about them may sometimes be daunting if you're new to the whole freelancing process. But you have to remember that this is a win-win situation: your clients don't need to spend time and money setting up for and training a new employee. So don't be frightened to ask for a decent pay.

3. Learn from the pros

Once you've narrowed down your focus and calculated how much you'd need to charge for your services to make them feasible, it's time to get some inspiration from the pros.

There are folks out there that have turned this into successful jobs and are earning thousands of dollars doing it every month. Try networking with other VAs, reading their blogs, and listening to podcasts on establishing a VA firm.

Are you only intending to make this a side-hustle? That's good, too. Side hustles are what helped me gain financial independence at the age of 30, so I'm pleased for you! Find out more about how to develop a prosperous side company.

You may desire to take a virtual assistant training course to discover the ins and outs of working as a VA so that you'd know precisely what to anticipate.

4. Build your internet presence

As a virtual assistant, you'll be giving an online service – so your consumers need to be satisfied that you're proficient at these things. That suggests you need a strong internet presence. To become visible to your consumers – and to grab their attention.

If you want prospective consumers to know about your services, you'll need a website or maybe even a blog. That, of course, will rely on the type of services you decide to supply. However, having an internet presence is vital for anybody looking to create a lucrative virtual assistant firm.

5. Start searching for your first job

Searching for your first job is thrilling – and, honestly, extremely scary. The fact is, you have to anticipate a few 'No, thank yous' along the path. Or to be overlooked now and again. Every freelancer goes through it. The most important thing is to remain persistent – and not take it personally.

And now, let me tell you where to locate that first probable customer!

Legally Protect Your Business

It is crucial to have an iron-clad virtual assistant contract consumers sign before working with you.

This isn't a lengthy document and I propose obtaining a lawyer to generate one for you instead than preparing one yourself. The free versions accessible online are either too long (clients are seeking to engage you to save time, you won't be aiding with your textbook-sized contract) or simply not complete enough.

You may purchase some wonderful virtual assistant contracts online anywhere from $200 and more. I recognize that you are striving to create money online and don't have $200 (or more) lying around. Your contract should cover the main things below and a dozen more:

Work Overview

I did this improperly from the beginning. This made me execute a lot of labor for free. Don't make the mistake of not properly stating what you'll be doing. Don't give space for assumptions, please. You'll regret it like I did. Take time to present a description of the job you are going to do for your customer so they know what they are paying for and not pass on unneeded work to you.

Payment Terms

Don't play with this, please. You need to precisely define how much you will be paid for each service you perform, how you will be paid (payment structure and specifications) When they'll get your invoice, and when payment is due.

Non-Disclosure Agreement

No doubt working as a virtual assistant might require your client to allow you access to sensitive information like their passwords, marketing plan, and customer's personal information. As a virtual assistant, you'll need to correctly advise your consumer about how you retain their information and essentially develop a non-disclosure agreement so they may have their piece of mind.

Termination Notification

Like any relationship, dealing with certain consumers may not be practical. You may need to split ways with certain consumers and it isn't pretty if you don't plan in advance. You'd need to submit what is considered a termination notice in your papers. This notification contains information concerning payment at the time of termination, who may file for termination, and how it will be delivered. Trust me, you don't want to accomplish your assignment and your customer chooses to cancel your appointment because they don't want to pay.

Independent Contractor Agreement

You need to be considered as a company owner as you work with clients and not for them. You're not their employee but an autonomous business partner answering their expectations, so you need to be treated as such.

Non-Solicitation Clause

This is a vital document you need to take care of. Some customers will not want you to publicize your services to their clientele. Even if you aren't in the same niche.

So they might offer you a non-solicitation agreement and ask you to sign. It is crucial to read it properly and have a lawyer review it before you do. Why? Because it may sometimes be extremely broad. So if you supply one in your welcome package, you'd set them at ease and they may not need to present you with their own more stringent evidence.

Level Up

Imagine you're a customer seeking for a virtual assistant mainly to manage your company's social media accounts, among some other fundamental marketing administration chores. You post a job on a freelance site like Upwork, and within a day, you get a dozen applications. When examining each prospect, what sort of things are you going to be searching for?

Past employment experience will always be one of the top reasons organizations choose to recruit someone. So any knowledge in the field, even if it's modest, may surely make your application stand out.

If you have no experience whatsoever, a wonderful approach to verify competency in a certain area is via free or low-cost certificates. Some prominent organizations and colleges provide something along the lines of a free certification program.

A few worth looking into are:

- Google Project Management: Professional Certificate
- Facebook Certified Digital Marketing Associate
- Microsoft Office Specialist: Outlook Associate
- Graphic Design Specialization from CalArts
- QuickBooks Certification
- SalesForces Administrator

When you add a certification from a respected firm (which can generally be done in roughly half a workday), you differentiate yourself from other novice candidates. It's something we can't advocate strongly enough.

Build A Brand

After you've chosen what work you'd want to perform you need to settle on your business name and build your branding and logo. I started off with such a simple VA website but later changed it. So you don't wait till everything is perfect - just get going!

You need to have a decent online look as your website and social media profiles WILL be inspected by prospective customers, but your primary objective is to attract clients and not faff around getting caught up in useless design details and never truly complete any work.

Final Words

So, there you have it. Not only is being a virtual assistant a flexible way to earn more money without leaving the comfort of your home but, if you're prepared to put in the work, it can become a lucrative vocation that you can pursue from anywhere in the world! The frequent blunder made by many VAs (and by all freelancers) is bypassing all those steps and jumping on sites like Upwork to start seeking for assignments.

This kind of freelancer often exits in disgust fairly shortly after beginning, whining about how competitive the sector is or how little money can be gained. Few VAs (and few freelancers in general) take the time to research what type of services consumers value most or to set up a complete résumé and service offering.

If you've followed each of the steps above, you'll have positioned yourself to get hired as a virtual assistant – even on the most competitive platforms. More crucially, you'll be able to start creating money from home without having to work for less than you're genuinely worth. You may not have the vital attributes necessary to become a Virtual Assistant but after reading this essay, you at least now have a better idea of what's involved and what to do next if you still feel it's something you may want to pursue.

Bonuses

Landing Your First Client

Why the first client? Because that's all it takes. When you follow these procedures to obtain your first customer, you can always utilize them to get your second or twentieth customer!

Tell your friends and family what you do: Chances are if they don't need your services, they'd at least know a small company owner who does.

Try cold pitching: Look out for possible customers and offer your services to them.

Ask for references: Remember the 2-to 3 folks you worked for in return for testimonials? Ask them for references. They might know someone who needs your services or needs them for themselves.

Prepare your VA resume and bid for jobs on LinkedIn: This is the first place most employers will look.

Bid for assignments on freelancing services like Upwork, Fiverr, and Indeed. Engage in LinkedIn, WhatsApp, Facebook groups, and other social media platforms and be valuable. People will notice.

Connect with other Virtual Assistants nearby, and ask them for sub-contract jobs. Attend events and network.

Available Opportunities as A VA

Freelance Marketplaces

Sites like Upwork and Total, provide hundreds of current jobs for all forms of virtual assistant employment. In many circumstances, you're competing with international talent, hence the costs tend to be cheaper. Nonetheless, there are some quite great consumers to be found on both sites.

Job Search Sites

Sites like FlexJobs, Indeed, Belay Solutions, Fancy Hands, and Zirtual provide various jobs for virtual assistants. You'll notice that bigger firms want to utilize established job platforms like these to seek staff. Because of this, they're normally hunting for individuals with some specialists who can work defined hours.

Fiverr

The second-largest freelancing marketplace is another option to consider. However, I see it as a category of its own as instead of browsing over work given by customers, you develop freelance projects that consumers may acquire on demand.

So, for example, a virtual assistant who specialized in social media may build jobs for producing banners, composing tweets, researching hashtags, and so on.

In that way, it's a good chance to test out demand for a variety of different activities and see what generates the most traction. When something does strike, it's a clue that there could be available potential to specialize in that sector.

Virtual Assistant Agencies

These agencies employ virtual assistants and then have them work for their customers. It's a good choice for folks with some experience desiring to work closer to a full-time workweek.

Go Get 'Em

I hope you've learned one or two things reading this book. If you have, make sure to leave a rating and/or review on the Amazon store. It goes a long way for indie authors like me. Thank you for buying this book.